From Your Friends At **The MAIL**

MARCH

A MONTH OF REPRODUCIBLES AT YOUR FINGERTIPS!

Grades 2–3

Editor:
Darcy Brown

Writers:
Darcy Brown, Susan Hohbach Walker

Art Coordinator:
Clevell Harris

Artists:
Pam Crane, Teresa Davidson, Nick Greenwood,
Clevell Harris, Sheila Krill, Mary Lester,
Rob Mayworth, Rebecca Saunders,
Barry Slate

Cover Artist:
Jennifer Tipton Bennett

©1998 by THE EDUCATION CENTER, INC.
All rights reserved.
ISBN #1-56234-231-2

Manufactured in the United States

10 9 8 7 6 5 4 3 2 1

Table Of Contents

March Free-Time

Monday	Tuesday	Wednesday	Thursday	Friday
The first day in March is National Pig Day. Write a story about your favorite pig in literature.	National Shoe Week is celebrated during the first week in March. Design and illustrate a picture of a new shoe style you would like to have.	Alexander Graham Bell, inventor of the telephone, was born on March 3, 1847. Write a paragraph that tells why a telephone is important in your life.	The first full week in March is National School Breakfast Week. Write a recipe for your favorite breakfast.	Make a bookmark in honor of Return The Borrowed Books Week, March 1–7. Then use it to remind yourself to return your library book to school.
In celebration of Aunts' Day on March 8, draw a picture of your favorite aunt, uncle, or other family member.	The planet Uranus was discovered on March 13, 1781. Can you name eight other planets?	March 14 is Save A Spider Day. Draw a picture of a place you might find a spider.	St. Patrick's Day is an Irish holiday that is celebrated on March 17. Write a story about a tiny leprechaun.	Four-leaf clovers are said to bring good luck. List some other well-known good-luck charms.
The first day of spring is March 20. List some things you do when spring is here.	Remember that March 21 is Memory Day. List some things you are asked to memorize. 4, 6, 12 9, 3, 2	March can be windy, which makes it perfect for Let's Go Fly A Kite Month. Design a paper kite to celebrate this month.	What holiday is it today? You decide! March 26 is Make Up Your Own Holiday Day. Draw a picture of your new holiday on drawing paper.	The Slinky®, a famous toy, was patented in March of 1947. Draw a toy that you would like to see created.
March is American Red Cross Month. List some ways you would like to help friends or neighbors in need.	Teacher Appreciation Day is celebrated on March 29. Design a card for your teacher to show your appreciation for him or her.	The first pencil with an eraser top was patented on March 30, 1858, by Hyman Lipman. Write a story about the biggest pencil in the world!	March 30 is also Doctors' Day, and the red carnation is the flower that is used to honor doctors. Draw a picture of a red carnation; then give it to a doctor you know.	The Eiffel Tower was officially opened to the public on March 31, 1889. List other buildings or landmarks that you have visited or seen in photographs.

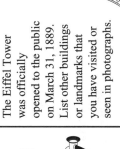
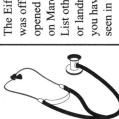

©1998 The Education Center, Inc. • *March Monthly Reproducibles* • Grades 2–3 • TEC945

Note To The Teacher: Have each student staple a copy of this page inside a file folder. Direct students to store their completed work in their folders.

3

March
Events And Activities For The Family

Directions: Select at least one activity below to complete as a family by the end of March.
(Challenge: See if your family can complete all three activities.)

National Nutrition Month®

Introduce your family to good nutrition when you celebrate National Nutrition Month®. Have family members cut pictures of healthful foods like breads, pasta, fruits, and vegetables from discarded magazines. Direct them to glue their pictures to a large piece of poster board. Display the poster in your kitchen or family room as a reminder to make healthful food choices. If desired, have your family work together once a week during March to prepare a healthful meal. Learning about good nutrition has never been more fun!

Birthday Of Ezra Jack Keats

Renowned children's author Ezra Jack Keats was born on March 11, 1916. Celebrate his birth by reading aloud one of his lovely picture books to your family.

- *Apartment Three* (Simon & Schuster Children's Division, 1986)
- *Goggles!* (Simon & Schuster Children's Division, 1987)
- *A Letter To Amy* (HarperCollins Children's Books, 1984)
- *John Henry: An American Legend* (Alfred A. Knopf Books For Young Readers, 1987)
- *The Snowy Day* (Puffin Books, 1976)
- *The Trip* (Greenwillow Books, 1978)

Flower Day

Observed annually on March 21, Flower Day provides a great opportunity for your family to promote the fun and creativity of planting flowers. Welcome this day with a one-of-a-kind planter. Gather the following supplies: white glue, a paintbrush, scissors, fabric scraps, a clay flowerpot, and clear spray-on shellac. Cut the fabric scraps into two- and three-inch squares. Next brush the squares with white glue and press them onto the pot. Continue to overlap the fabric squares until the pot is completely covered. When the glue has dried, spray a coat of shellac over the pot. Plant your favorite flowers in the patchwork pot, and then set it on a windowsill for everyone to enjoy!

In Like A Lion, Out Like A Lamb

Put this familiar phrase to good use as students participate in these one-of-a-kind ideas. You can count on your lambs and lions having plenty of fun!

Windy-Day Windsocks

Remind students that March comes in like a lion with these colorful windsocks! Provide each youngster with a copy of the windsock patterns on page 8. To make a windsock, a student rolls a 6" x 18" sheet of construction paper into a cylinder and glues the overlapping edges together as shown; then she sets the cylinder aside to dry. Next she colors and cuts out her windsock patterns and glues them to the cylinder once it has dried. Next she glues six 16-inch crepe-paper strips inside the lower rim of her project. She punches two holes near the top of the cylinder so that the holes are on opposite sides of the windsock (see illustration). She then threads a different end of a 16-inch length of yarn through each hole and secures it to the project by tying it. Invite students to suspend their windsocks around the classroom for all to enjoy!

Just The Facts

Teach your youngsters about lions and lambs with this informative booklet. Duplicate one copy of pages 6 and 7 (the booklet pattern and booklet pages) for each student. A student reads the fact on each booklet page; then he illustrates each page, and the booklet pattern, as desired. To complete his booklet, he cuts apart his booklet pages, assembles them in numerical order, and staples them to his booklet pattern as shown.

Lions
And
Lambs

What Does It Mean?

March is said to "come in like a lion and go out like a lamb." Help your youngsters understand what the expression means with this fun writing activity. Write the phrase on a sheet of chart paper and post it in a prominent location in your classroom. Invite a volunteer to read the phrase aloud to the class. Ask students to tell you what the first part of the phrase means; then write their responses on the chart. Repeat the procedure with the second part of the phrase. Next have each student use writing paper to write a fun story about a day that came in like a lion and went out like a lamb. Have students share their stories with their classmates. Collect the papers and bind them between two construction-paper covers. Title the booklet "In Like A Lion, Out Like A Lamb." Then place the booklet in the reading center for independent reading.

Booklet Pattern

Staple here.

Most sheep are found in pastures and on farms.

©1998 The Education Center, Inc.

Booklet Pages

Illustrated by _____

Lions and lambs are both mammals.

2

Lions
And
Lambs

©1998 The Education Center, Inc.

There are many interesting facts about lions and lambs.

1

Lions live in groups called *prides,*

6

Most lions can be found in grassy plains.

10

and lambs are members of the sheep family.

5

Sheep are quick-moving animals. They like to eat grasses, grains, and hay.

9

Lions are members of the cat family,

4

Lions are strong, powerful animals. They like to eat zebras, deer, and buffalo.

8

A baby lion is called a *cub.* A baby sheep is called a *lamb.*

3

and sheep live in groups called *flocks.*

7

©1998 The Education Center, Inc. • *March Monthly Reproducibles* • Grades 2–3 • TEC945

Note To The Teacher: Use with "Just The Facts" on page 5.

Windsock Patterns

Note To The Teacher: Use with "Windy-Day Windsocks" on page 5.

Name _____

King Of The Pride

Solve each addition problem.
Show your work.
Cross off each matching answer on the tree.

899	817	580
882	711	543
633	730	873
	974	

$$\begin{array}{r} 433 \\ + 466 \\ \hline \end{array} \qquad \begin{array}{r} 157 \\ + 725 \\ \hline \end{array} \qquad \begin{array}{r} 423 \\ + 328 \\ \hline \end{array} \qquad \begin{array}{r} 832 \\ + 158 \\ \hline \end{array}$$

$$\begin{array}{r} 126 \\ + 835 \\ \hline \end{array} \qquad \begin{array}{r} 575 \\ + 127 \\ \hline \end{array} \qquad \begin{array}{r} 264 \\ + 508 \\ \hline \end{array} \qquad \begin{array}{r} 415 \\ + 555 \\ \hline \end{array}$$

$$\begin{array}{r} 555 \\ + 156 \\ \hline \end{array} \qquad \begin{array}{r} 438 \\ + 529 \\ \hline \end{array} \qquad \begin{array}{r} 637 \\ + 236 \\ \hline \end{array} \qquad \begin{array}{r} 264 \\ + 196 \\ \hline \end{array} \qquad \begin{array}{r} 362 \\ + 549 \\ \hline \end{array}$$

$$\begin{array}{r} 172 \\ + 598 \\ \hline \end{array} \qquad \begin{array}{r} 416 \\ + 217 \\ \hline \end{array} \qquad \begin{array}{r} 578 \\ + 239 \\ \hline \end{array} \qquad \begin{array}{r} 319 \\ + 345 \\ \hline \end{array} \qquad \begin{array}{r} 376 \\ + 454 \\ \hline \end{array}$$

$$\begin{array}{r} 688 \\ + 155 \\ \hline \end{array} \qquad \begin{array}{r} 493 \\ + 199 \\ \hline \end{array} \qquad \begin{array}{r} 827 \\ + 147 \\ \hline \end{array} \qquad \begin{array}{r} 385 \\ + 195 \\ \hline \end{array} \qquad \begin{array}{r} 267 \\ + 276 \\ \hline \end{array}$$

$$\begin{array}{r} 459 \\ + 462 \\ \hline \end{array} \qquad \begin{array}{r} 348 \\ + 638 \\ \hline \end{array} \qquad \begin{array}{r} 495 \\ + 235 \\ \hline \end{array}$$

460
664
967
770
830
751
911
692
921
990
843
970
772
702
961
986

Bonus Box:
Choose ten
numbers on
the tree. Write
them in order
from *least* to
greatest on
the back of
this paper.

Name _____

Lovable Lambs

Solve each subtraction problem.
Show your work.
Cross off each matching answer on the bushes.

188	439	77
109	275	227
26	145	57
78	387	447

```
  405        702        602
- 217      - 335      - 327
```

```
  303        307        402
- 144      - 198      - 387
```

```
  101        507        104        906        604
-  75      - 138      -  47      -  88      - 165
```

```
  705        806        605        905        406
- 499      - 568      - 218      -  36      - 329
```

```
  204        707        802        203        901
- 126      - 358      - 496      -  58      - 454
```

```
             503        808        502
           - 276      - 319      - 244
```

238	15	159
869	367	206
369	489	818
306	349	258

Bonus Box: Write five more subtraction problems on the back of this sheet; then have a friend solve them.

10

St. Patrick's Day

St. Patrick's Day honors the man who introduced Christianity to Ireland about 1,550 years ago. St. Patrick is believed to have driven all the snakes out of Ireland, and there are no snakes there today. The legend of the leprechaun also dates back over 1,550 years. Some people believe that if a leprechaun is caught, he must reveal where a buried treasure lies.

Lucky Clovers

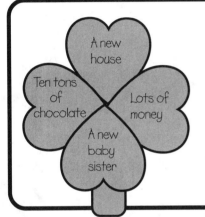

A new house
Ten tons of chocolate
Lots of money
A new baby sister

Bring the luck o' the Irish to your classroom with these lucky clovers! Tell students that a three-leafed clover called a *shamrock* grows everywhere in Ireland. The Irish believe that shamrocks protect a person from evil spirits, and they often carry them for good luck. A four-leaf clover is said to be even luckier—it brings twice the luck! After sharing this information, have each youngster make a lucky four-leaf clover. Each student will need a construction-paper copy of the patterns on page 17. To make his clover, have each child cut out the hearts and glue them to the stem as shown. When the glue has dried, have each youngster write four ways his clover could bring him good luck. Invite students to share their lucky clovers with their classmates. Then bring the luck o' the Irish to your classroom by displaying the shamrocks around the room for everyone to enjoy!

Leprechaun Magic

A little leprechaun magic will inspire your budding authors to write these magical stories! The day before St. Patrick's Day, after students have left for the day, arrange your classroom to look like leprechauns visited. To do this, tip over a couple of chairs, tape green "leprechaun" footprints on the wall around the chalkboard, and sprinkle gold glitter on the floor. After your students have witnessed the aftermath of the visit, have them pen leprechaun stories. Duplicate one copy of the pot and leprechaun patterns on page 18 for each student. Have each youngster write a magical leprechaun story on the pot pattern. Next have her cut out the pot pattern and glue it to a sheet of black construction paper; then have her trim the paper to create an eye-catching border. To complete her project, each student colors the leprechaun topper, cuts it out, and glues it atop her story. Invite youngsters to share their stories with their classmates. If desired, display the stories on a bulletin board titled "Leprechaun Magic."

One day my sister Sarah was walking in the forest. All of a sudden a magic leprechaun appeared. Sarah was so surprised! She chased the leprechaun and found his gold.
The End
Lucy

In The Green

Get your students in the green with this great St. Patrick's Day game! Duplicate one game card on page 16 for each student. To begin, ask youngsters to name some of their favorite green things. List their responses on the chalkboard. Then challenge students to learn about one another by playing In The Green. The object of the game is for each youngster to obtain as many signatures on his sheet as possible. Remind students that the statements must be true about themselves. Set a time limit (such as ten minutes) and let the game begin. When time has elapsed, have each youngster count the number of signatures he's collected. Select a few students to share interesting details about their classmates. Then reward all youngsters with a special treat, such as green apples or green jelly beans.

Shamrock Shenanigans

Color the shamrocks and the hearts green.
Cut out the hearts.
Put a dot of glue on each ●.
Match each antonym to a shamrock leaf.

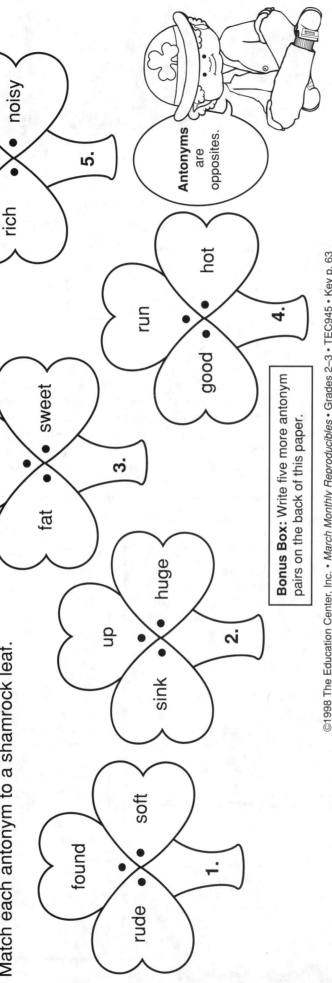

Antonyms are opposites.

5.

start ● noisy
rich

3.

in ● sweet
fat

4.

run ● hot
good

2.

up ● huge
sink

1.

found ● soft
rude

Bonus Box: Write five more antonym pairs on the back of this paper.

©1998 The Education Center, Inc. • *March Monthly Reproducibles* • Grades 2–3 • TEC945 • Key p. 63

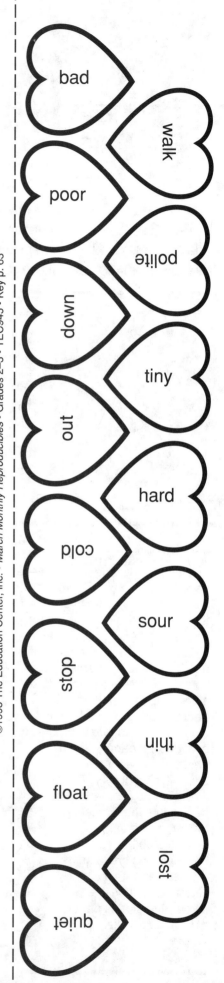

bad

walk

poor

polite

down

tiny

out

hard

cold

sour

stop

thin

float

lost

quiet

Name _____

Pick A Pattern

Study each pattern.
Draw what comes next in the last shamrock.

1.

2.

3.

4.

5.

6.

7.

8.

Bonus Box: Make your own shamrock pattern on the back of this paper.

Name _____

Lucky Pots Of Gold

Add the money on the pots.
Color the coins at the bottom of the page.
Cut out the coins and glue them above the answers.

1.   19¢
   + 66¢

2.   25¢
   + 25¢

3.   17¢
   + 28¢

4.   48¢
   + 44¢

5.   37¢
   + 52¢

6.   86¢
   + 9¢

7.   69¢
   + 21¢

8.   50¢
   + 29¢

9.   55¢
   + 18¢

10.   26¢
    + 37¢

11.   38¢
    + 34¢

12.   25¢
    + 68¢

79¢   63¢   90¢   73¢   50¢   93¢

92¢   89¢   45¢   72¢   95¢   85¢

Name _____

St. Patrick's Syllable Sprouts

Read the word on each potato.
Think of how many syllables are in the word.
Draw one sprout for each syllable on the potato.

Example:

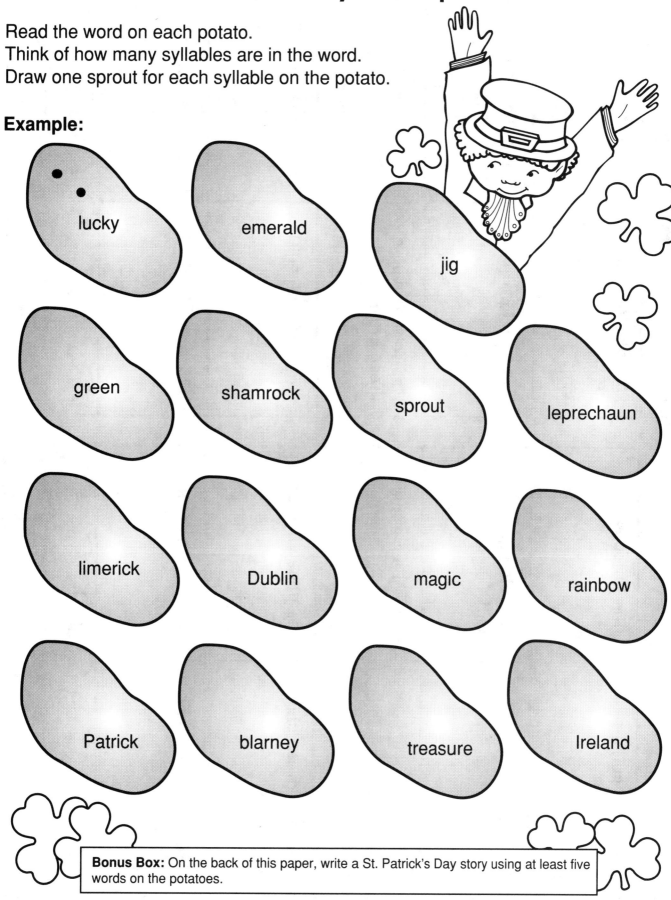

lucky

emerald

jig

green

shamrock

sprout

leprechaun

limerick

Dublin

magic

rainbow

Patrick

blarney

treasure

Ireland

Bonus Box: On the back of this paper, write a St. Patrick's Day story using at least five words on the potatoes.

Game Cards

In The Green

Favorite color is green	Likes broccoli	
Has tried kiwi	Has eaten green Jell-O®	
Has colored with a green crayon	Likes green apples	
Owns a green shirt	Has ridden in a green car	
Has read *Green Eggs And Ham*	Can name a green plant	

©1998 The Education Center, Inc. • *March Monthly Reproducibles* • Grades 2–3 • TEC945

In The Green

Favorite color is green	Likes broccoli	
Has tried kiwi	Has eaten green Jell-O®	
Has colored with a green crayon	Likes green apples	
Owns a green shirt	Has ridden in a green car	
Has read *Green Eggs And Ham*	Can name a green plant	

©1998 The Education Center, Inc. • *March Monthly Reproducibles* • Grades 2–3 • TEC945

Note To The Teacher: Use with "In The Green" on page 11.

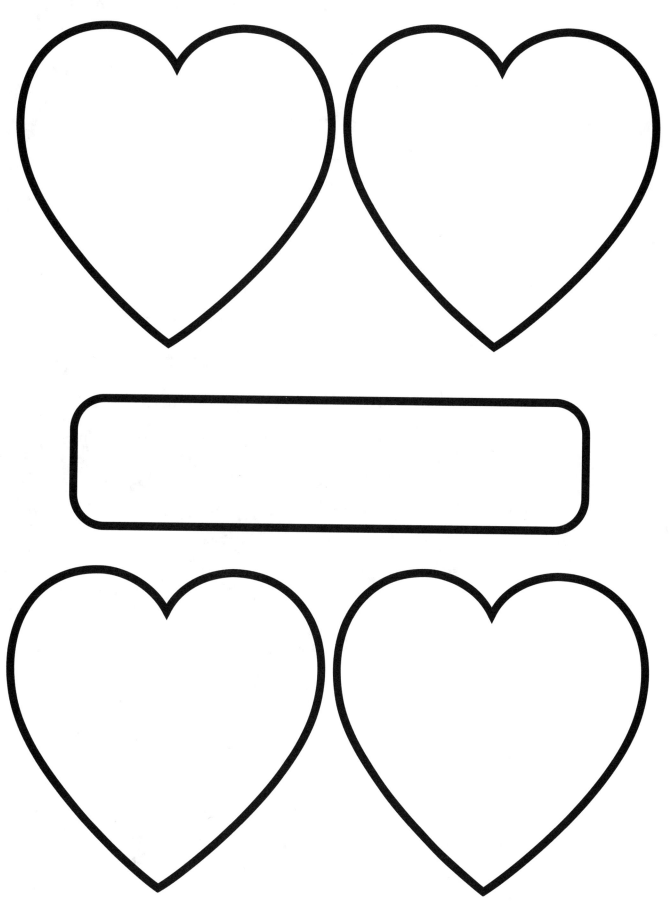

Note To The Teacher: Use with "Lucky Clovers" on page 11.

Pot Pattern

Leprechaun Topper

Note To The Teacher: Use with "Leprechaun Magic" on page 11.

NATIONAL PEANUT MONTH

Your students won't be able to resist these mouthwatering activities when they celebrate National Peanut Month in March.

The Peanut Man

This student-made booklet will introduce your youngsters to George Washington Carver. To begin, copy the facts to the right onto a sheet of chart paper; then post them in a visible location in your classroom. Next duplicate one tan construction-paper copy of the peanut book pattern on page 20 for each student. To make his booklet, a youngster traces his pattern onto five sheets of white paper and cuts them out. Next he copies each fact onto a different peanut cutout; then he illustrates each fact as desired. To complete his booklet, he writes his name on the front cover and then staples the pages in order behind it. Invite students to take their completed booklets home to share with family members.

- George Washington Carver was born a slave in 1864 on a farm near Diamond, Missouri.
- When George was young, he liked plants and he liked to learn.
- In 1891, George went to college to earn a degree in agriculture.
- Soon after college, George became head of the Tuskegee Institute agricultural department.
- George began to research peanuts. He made more than 300 products from peanuts.

Peanut Practice

What better way to practice basic skills than with this tasty center! Duplicate construction-paper copies of the elephant and peanut patterns on page 22 and cut them out. Program the elephants with word problems and the peanuts with corresponding answers. Then laminate the pieces for durability. Place the programmed pieces and a supply of whole (unshelled) peanuts at a learning center. To use the center, a student reads the problem on an elephant, uses the whole peanuts to find the answer, and matches the correct programmed peanut to its elephant. For even more practice, program the elephants with synonyms, antonyms, or basic addition or subtraction facts; then write each corresponding word or math answer on a matching peanut.

Joe bought a box of 20 peanuts. He gave 3 to Sue. How many peanuts are left in the box?

"Peanutty" Recipes

Review writing skills when students write their own "peanutty" recipes. Ask students if they can name the most popular product made from peanuts (peanut butter). Tell them that they will each be writing a recipe using peanut butter as one ingredient. To prepare for the writing activity, have youngsters name words used when writing a recipe—like *stir, mix, cup, bowl,* and *spoon*—and list them on the chalkboard. Next duplicate one copy of the recipe card on page 21 for each student. A youngster thinks of a name for her recipe and writes it on the top line. Next she lists the ingredients; then she writes the directions using the words from the list. To complete the project, she glues her recipe to a slightly larger sheet of construction paper and trims the paper to create a border. Have students share their recipes with their classmates; then display them on a bulletin board titled " 'Peanutty' Recipes."

Peanut Book Pattern

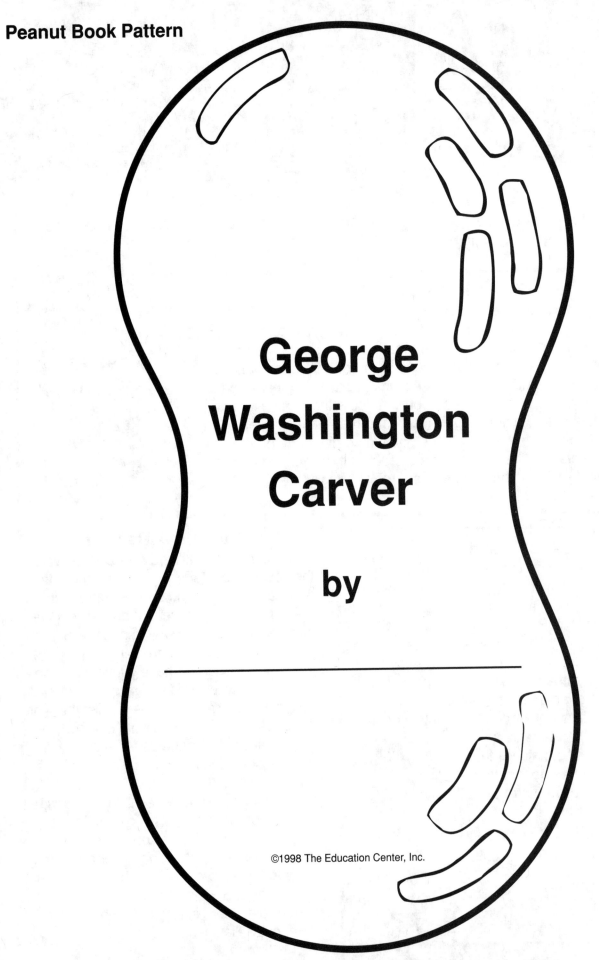

George Washington Carver

by

_____

©1998 The Education Center, Inc.

Note To The Teacher: Use with "The Peanut Man" on page 19.

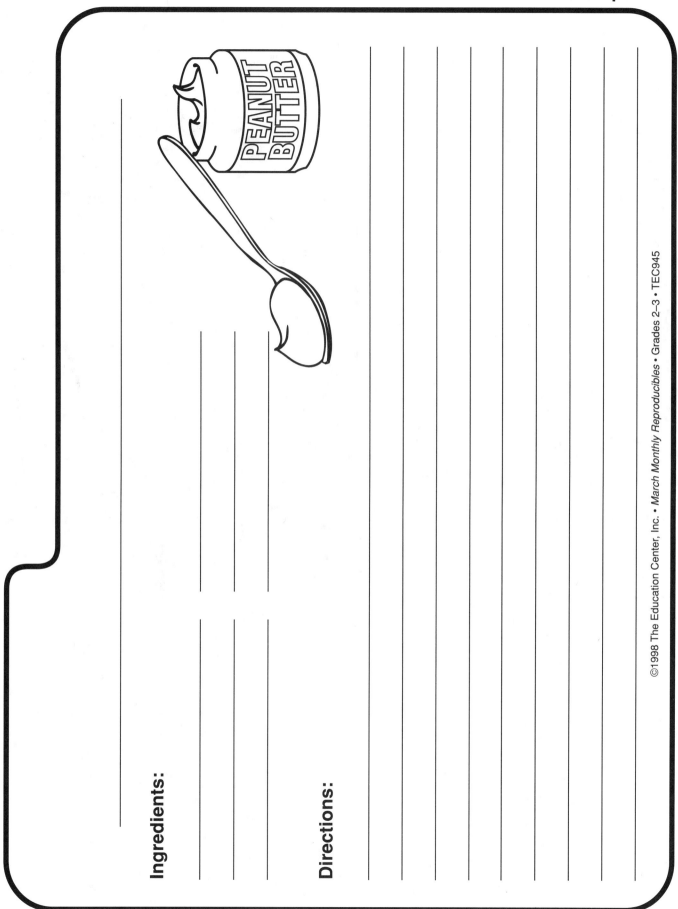

Ingredients:

Directions:

©1998 The Education Center, Inc. • *March Monthly Reproducibles* • Grades 2–3 • TEC945

Note To The Teacher: Use with " 'Peanutty' Recipes" on page 19.

Elephant And Peanut Patterns

Note To The Teacher: Use with "Peanut Practice" on page 19.

National Peanut Month
Multiplication review

Follow The Peanut Trail

Help the elephant find its way to the circus tent.

Write what's missing in each ☐ .

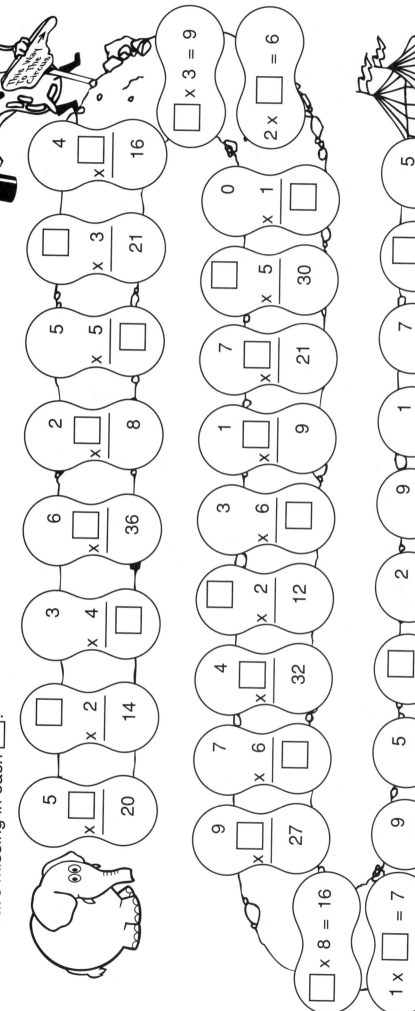

☐ x 3 = 9

2 x ☐ = 6

$\begin{array}{r} 4 \\ \times\ \square \\ \hline 16 \end{array}$

$\begin{array}{r} \square \\ \times\ 3 \\ \hline 21 \end{array}$

$\begin{array}{r} 5 \\ \times\ 5 \\ \hline \square \end{array}$

$\begin{array}{r} 2 \\ \times\ \square \\ \hline 8 \end{array}$

$\begin{array}{r} 6 \\ \times\ \square \\ \hline 36 \end{array}$

$\begin{array}{r} 3 \\ \times\ 4 \\ \hline \square \end{array}$

$\begin{array}{r} \square \\ \times\ 2 \\ \hline 14 \end{array}$

$\begin{array}{r} 5 \\ \times\ \square \\ \hline 20 \end{array}$

$\begin{array}{r} 0 \\ \times\ 1 \\ \hline \square \end{array}$

$\begin{array}{r} \square \\ \times\ 5 \\ \hline 30 \end{array}$

$\begin{array}{r} 7 \\ \times\ \square \\ \hline 21 \end{array}$

$\begin{array}{r} 1 \\ \times\ \square \\ \hline 9 \end{array}$

$\begin{array}{r} 3 \\ \times\ 6 \\ \hline \square \end{array}$

$\begin{array}{r} \square \\ \times\ 2 \\ \hline 12 \end{array}$

$\begin{array}{r} 4 \\ \times\ \square \\ \hline 32 \end{array}$

$\begin{array}{r} 7 \\ \times\ 6 \\ \hline \square \end{array}$

$\begin{array}{r} 9 \\ \times\ \square \\ \hline 27 \end{array}$

☐ x 8 = 16

1 x ☐ = 7

$\begin{array}{r} 5 \\ \times\ \square \\ \hline 45 \end{array}$

$\begin{array}{r} \square \\ \times\ 2 \\ \hline 10 \end{array}$

$\begin{array}{r} 7 \\ \times\ \square \\ \hline 35 \end{array}$

$\begin{array}{r} 1 \\ \times\ \square \\ \hline 3 \end{array}$

$\begin{array}{r} 9 \\ \times\ 2 \\ \hline \square \end{array}$

$\begin{array}{r} 2 \\ \times\ \square \\ \hline 4 \end{array}$

$\begin{array}{r} \square \\ \times\ 8 \\ \hline 56 \end{array}$

$\begin{array}{r} 5 \\ \times\ \square \\ \hline 5 \end{array}$

$\begin{array}{r} 9 \\ \times\ \square \\ \hline 81 \end{array}$

Bonus Box: On the back of this page, write a story about an elephant that joins the circus.

©1998 The Education Center, Inc. • *March Monthly Reproducibles* • Grades 2–3 • TEC945 • Key p. 63

Calling All Peanuts!

Read the word on each peanut.
Write its rhyming word on the line.
Cross off each word on the elephant as you use it.

1. join _____

2. bright _____

3. sleep _____

4. caught _____

5. stream _____

6. kind _____

7. string _____

8. stain _____

9. pickle _____

10. clown _____

11. broom _____

12. chair _____

13. flower _____

14. thread _____

15. coat _____

16. stable _____

brown   find
main   peep
spread   stair
knight   gleam
float   coin
groom   power
spring   tickle
taught   cable

Bonus Box: Write five more pairs of
rhyming words on the back of this page.

Colorful Kites AND Wild Wind

March brings spring and *lots* of wild and windy weather. Capitalize on these blustery days by having your youngsters participate in this breezy collection of activities.

Wind Is...

These colorful kites will have your students in-the-know with descriptive words! Take your class outside on a sunny, windy day. Ask students to observe the wind and think of words to describe it, such as *breezy, whipping, rustling,* and *whistling.* When you return to the classroom, list the students' responses on the chalkboard. Then have each youngster make a descriptive kite. Duplicate one white construction-paper copy of page 27 for each student. Have him complete the sentence "Wind is…" by writing a different word to describe wind on each bow; then have him write his name in the blank on the kite pattern. Next direct the student to color and cut out his kite and bows. Have each youngster tape an 18-inch length of yarn (the tail) to the bottom of his kite; then have him evenly tape each bow to the tail. Invite each student to share his colorful kite with his classmates. Collect the kites and display them around the room for adjective skills that really soar!

Words In The Wind

Have your students create a windy word bank for writing practice. At the beginning of March, cut a large cloud or kite shape from bulletin-board paper. Ask students to brainstorm words and phrases that contain the word *wind*—like *windmill, windsock,* and *wind chime.* Write each response on the cutout. Then display the cutout in a location visible to all students. Have each student write a story about a topic like "The Best Windy Day Ever!" Encourage each youngster to use some of the words and phrases in her writing. Challenge students to add additional words and phrases to the word bank throughout the month of March. If desired, continue the practice for the remainder of the school year with different monthly cutouts.

Uplifting Airplanes

Involve your youngsters in an airplane-flying contest to provide practice with following directions. Copy the steps to the right onto a large sheet of paper and display it on the chalkboard. Distribute one sheet of drawing paper to each student. Direct him to fold his paper by following the plane-making steps. Then take your class outside for an airplane-flying contest. Have each student, in turn, fly his plane from a starting point. Mark the position of each plane's landing with a personalized craft stick. Reward your youngsters for the *longest flight,* the *shortest flight,* and the *wildest flight.* Your students will be in for a windfall of wondrous fun!

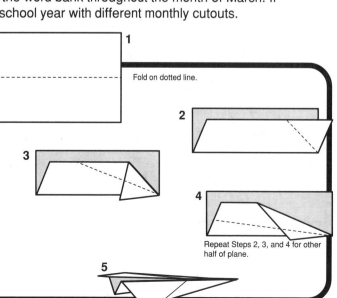

Name _____

High-Flying Fun!

Cut out the bows.
Glue each bow on the correct kite tail.
Color the kites and bows.

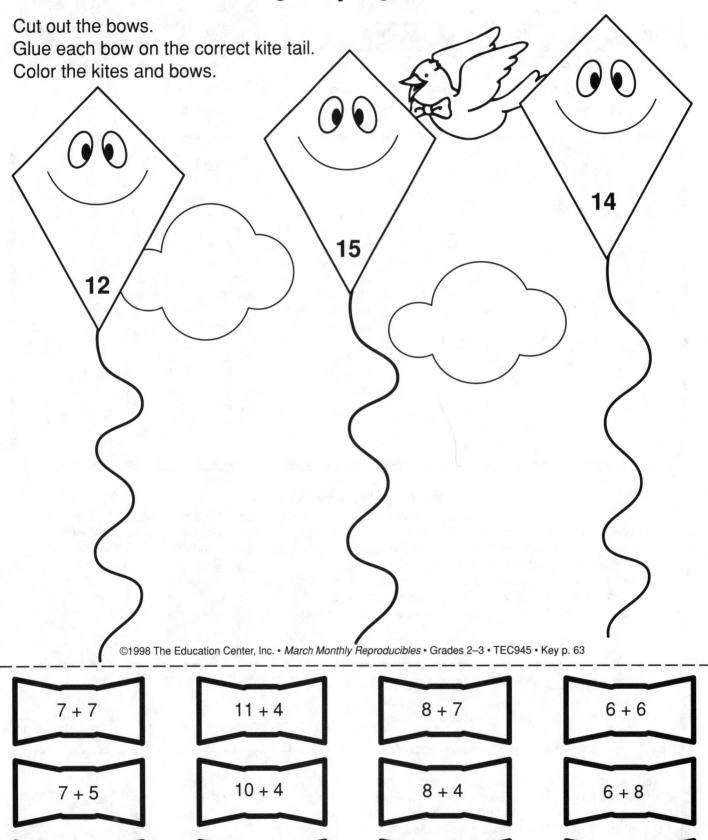

12

15

14

©1998 The Education Center, Inc. • *March Monthly Reproducibles* • Grades 2–3 • TEC945 • Key p. 63

7 + 7	11 + 4	8 + 7	6 + 6
7 + 5	10 + 4	8 + 4	6 + 8
6 + 9	9 + 3	9 + 5	10 + 5

Wind
is...

name

Note To The Teacher: Use with "Wind Is…" on page 25.

Let's Go Fly A Kite!

Read the sentences below.
Cut out the sentences.
Glue them in order in the boxes.

1.

2.

3.

4.

5.

6.

7.

8.

Meg held the kite, while Tim let out the string.	Meg and Tim asked their mom if they could fly a kite outside.
It was a sunny and windy day.	The kite flew high in the air.
Meg let go of the kite as Tim started to run.	They took the kite to the park.
Meg and Tim got the kite out of the garage.	The wind caught the kite.

Name _____

Time To Fly

Read the clock on each kite.
Write the time on the line below the kite.

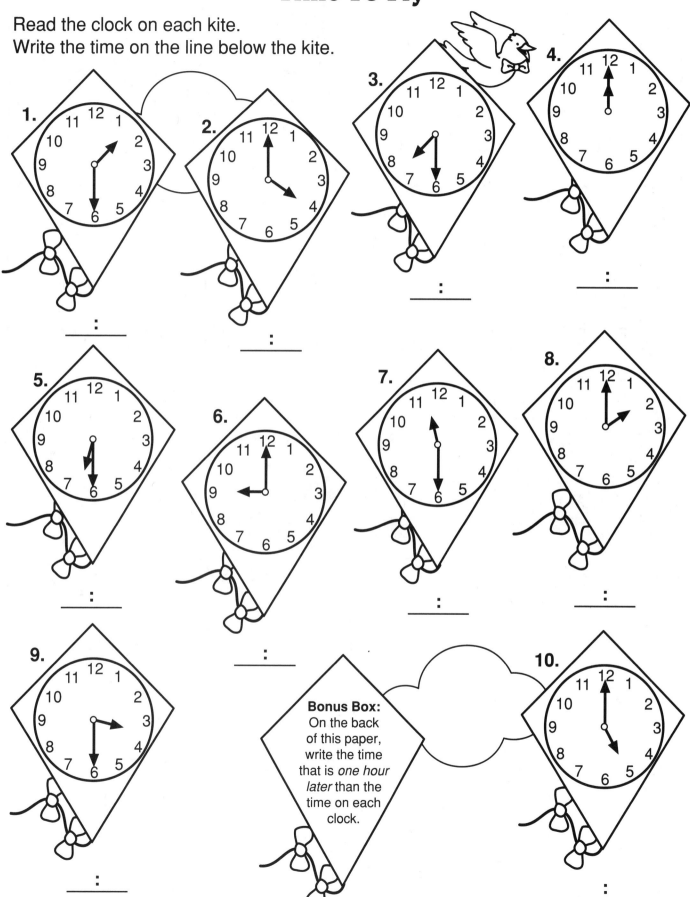

1. ____ : ____

2. ____ : ____

3. ____ : ____

4. ____ : ____

5. ____ : ____

6. ____ : ____

7. ____ : ____

8. ____ : ____

9. ____ : ____

Bonus Box:
On the back of this paper, write the time that is *one hour later* than the time on each clock.

10. ____ : ____

Lift Up Your Life With Books!

Catch The Wind!
All About Kites
by Gail Gibbons
Little, Brown And Company; 1989

Dancing With The Wind
by Stanton Orser
Northland Publishing Company, 1997

Mirandy And Brother Wind
by Patricia C. McKissack
Random House Books For Young
Readers, 1997

Moonlight Kite
by Helen E. Buckley
Lothrop, Lee & Shepard Books; 1997

The Wind Garden
by Angela McAllister
and Claire Fletcher
Lothrop, Lee & Shepard Books; 1995

©1998 The Education Center, Inc.

Soar Into The Sky With Books!

Catch The Wind!
All About Kites
by Gail Gibbons
Little, Brown And Company; 1989

Dancing With The Wind
by Stanton Orser
Northland Publishing Company, 1997

Mirandy And Brother Wind
by Patricia C. McKissack
Random House Books For Young
Readers, 1997

Moonlight Kite
by Helen E. Buckley
Lothrop, Lee & Shepard Books; 1997

The Wind Garden
by Angela McAllister
and Claire Fletcher
Lothrop, Lee & Shepard Books; 1995

©1998 The Education Center, Inc.

The Sky's The Limit With Books

Catch The Wind!
All About Kites
by Gail Gibbons
Little, Brown And Company; 1989

Dancing With The Wind
by Stanton Orser
Northland Publishing Company, 1997

Mirandy And Brother Wind
by Patricia C. McKissack
Random House Books For Young
Readers, 1997

Moonlight Kite
by Helen E. Buckley
Lothrop, Lee & Shepard Books; 1997

The Wind Garden
by Angela McAllister
and Claire Fletcher
Lothrop, Lee & Shepard Books; 1995

Up, Up, And Away With Books!

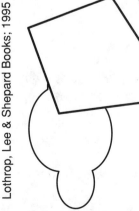

©1998 The Education Center, Inc.

Note To The Teacher: Duplicate the bookmarks on construction paper, cut them out, and distribute them to your students. Encourage each youngster to read one of the titles on his bookmark.

POP! POP! POP!

This cache of bubble gum ideas and reproducibles will have your youngsters bursting with excitement!

GUM

Gumball Goodies

These sweet story maps are just what you need to enhance your reading program. Each student will need a copy of the story map on page 32. To begin, assign students a story or book that you have read as a class (or have each youngster select a story she has read independently). To complete her map, a student writes the appropriate information from her story in the correct places on her gumball machine. Then she gives her recommendation of the story by writing the number of gumballs she thinks it deserves in the blank. She colors the gumballs on her map, cuts out her map, and then glues it to a slightly larger sheet of colored construction paper. Collect the story maps and mount them on a wall or bulletin board with the title "Gumball Goodies."

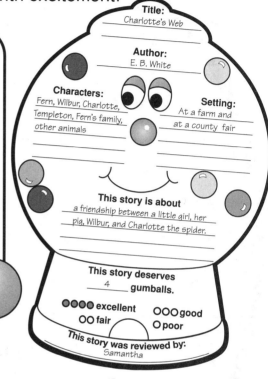

Title: Charlotte's Web

Author: E. B. White

Characters: Fern, Wilbur, Charlotte, Templeton, Fern's family, other animals

Setting: At a farm and at a county fair

This story is about a friendship between a little girl, her pig, Wilbur, and Charlotte the spider.

This story deserves 4 **gumballs.**

●●●● excellent ○○○ good
○○ fair ○ poor

This story was reviewed by: Samantha

Chewing Gum Favorites

Have your youngsters review graphing skills with this flavorful chewing gum graph. Purchase different flavors of gum, like mint, cinnamon, and fruit. (Make sure you have a class supply of each flavor.) Draw a bar graph outline on a large piece of poster board; then label the graph accordingly. To complete the graph, have each student sample each flavor of gum and attach a personalized gum cutout in the column of his favorite. Evaluate the resulting graph with the class. To extend the lesson, have students sample and graph their favorite brands of sugarless chewing gum or bubble gum.

GUM

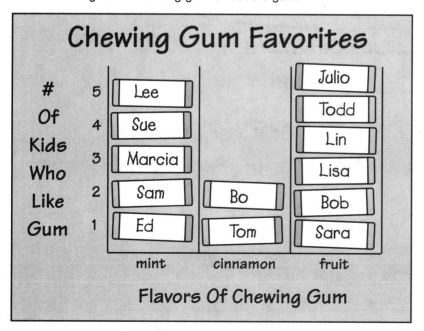

Chewing Gum Favorites

# Of Kids Who Like Gum		mint	cinnamon	fruit
5		Lee		Julio
4		Sue		Todd
3		Marcia		Lin
2		Sam	Bo	Lisa
1		Ed	Tom	Bob
				Sara

Flavors Of Chewing Gum

How Long Does It Last?

Challenge students to determine how long the flavor in a piece of bubble gum lasts with this exciting experiment! Provide each youngster with a piece of two popular brands of bubble gum. Designate one kind "Brand A" and the other "Brand B." Tell students that they will be chewing the gum to find out how long the flavor lasts. At your signal, have each student unwrap his piece of Brand A gum and begin chewing it. Instruct each youngster to give a thumbs-up sign when his gum has lost its flavor. When the last child gives a thumbs-up sign, write down the total amount of time it took on the chalkboard. Then repeat the activity with the other brand of bubble gum. Compare the times it took for each gum to lose its flavor.

Story Map Pattern

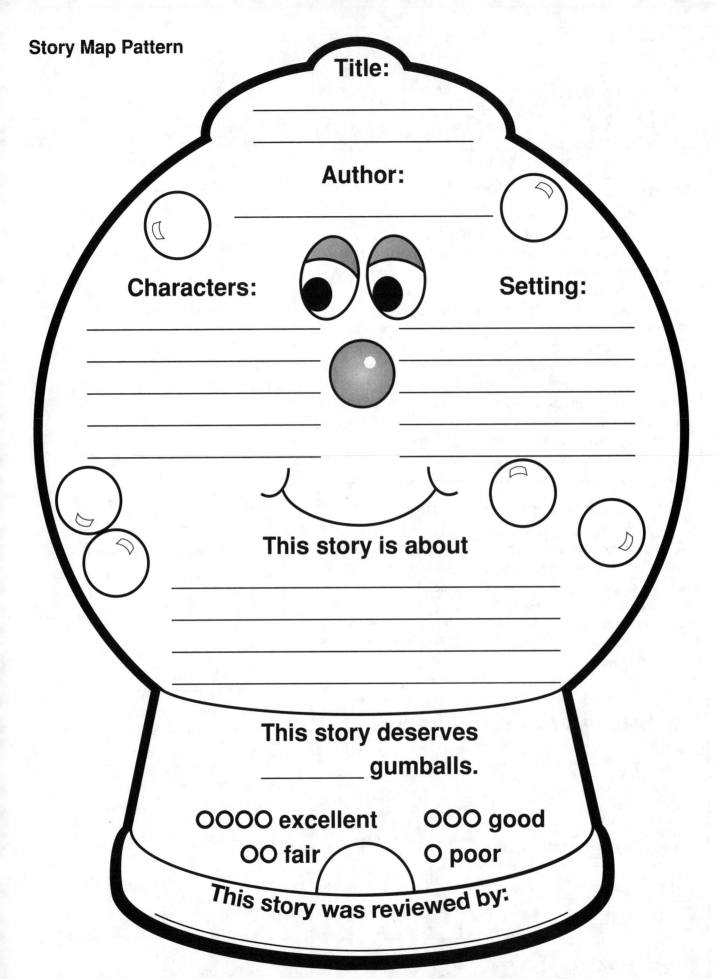

Title:

_____

_____

Author:

_____

Characters: Setting:

_____   _____

_____   _____

_____   _____

_____   _____

This story is about

_____

_____

_____

_____

This story deserves

_____ **gumballs.**

OOOO **excellent**   OOO **good**

OO **fair**   O **poor**

This story was reviewed by:

_____

©1998 The Education Center, Inc. • *March Monthly Reproducibles* • Grades 2–3 • TEC945

32   **Note To The Teacher:** Use with "Gumball Goodies" on page 31.

Name _____

Great Gumballs!

Read each word problem.
Solve each problem on the back of this page.
Write the answer in the blank. Then color the correct gumball.

1. Susan bought 48 pieces of gum on Thursday. By Saturday she had chewed 9 pieces. How many pieces of gum does Susan have left?

   _____

2. Kiesha bought 3 packs of peppermint gum. Each pack cost 25¢. How much money did Kiesha spend? _____

3. Lin has 12 gumballs. Meg has 19. How many gumballs do Lin and Meg have altogether?

   _____

4. Eric bought 2 packs of gum at the store. Each pack of gum has 14 sticks. How many sticks in all? _____

5. Molly had 50 gumballs. She gave 23 of them to Sam. How many gumballs does Molly have left? _____

6. Raj has 80¢ to spend on gum. How many 10¢ gumballs can Raj buy at the candy store?

   _____

7. Tim has 18 sticks of gum, Ed has 20 sticks of gum, and Kevin has 14 sticks of gum. How many sticks of gum do Tim, Ed, and Kevin have altogether? _____

8. Jeff had 75¢. He bought a pack of gum for 25¢. How much change will Jeff get back? _____

9. Josh bought 33 gumballs at the store. He gave his sister 9 gumballs. How many gumballs does Josh have left? _____

10. Julio had 95¢ to spend at the market. He bought a pack of mint gum for 49¢. How much money does Julio have left? _____

Name _____

Soft 'n' Chewy

Read the words on each piece of gum.
Write the words in ABC order on the lines.

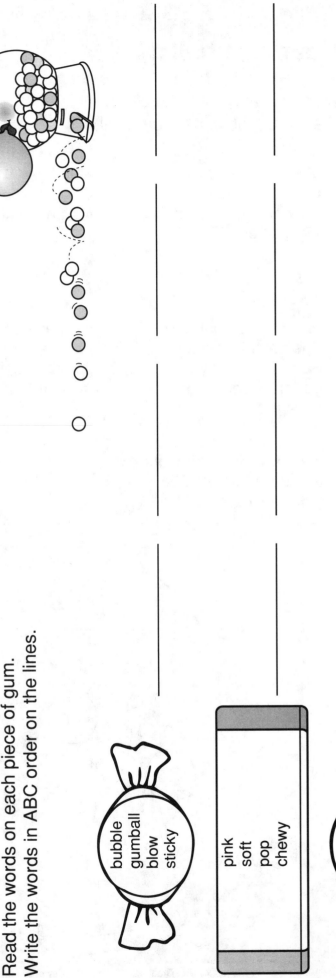

bubble
gumball
blow
sticky

_____

_____

_____

_____

pink
soft
pop
chewy

_____

_____

_____

_____

wrapper
cinnamon
candy
brand

_____

_____

_____

_____

super
minty
tasty
messy

_____

_____

_____

_____

Bonus Box: On the back of this page, write a bubble gum story using at least five words from above.

SEE HOW THEY GROW!

Invite your youngsters to discover the wonder in plants with this blooming collection of activities!

Plants, Plants, Plants!

Challenge students to keep track of plant growth with these informative booklets. Each student will need one copy of pages 36, 37, and 38. To make his booklet, each youngster cuts apart his booklet pages and compiles them in sequential order. Next he staples them along the left edge behind the booklet cover; then he writes his name in the blank.

Next give each student a seed. Direct him to examine his seed; then have him complete page 1 in his booklet. Next instruct him to plant his seed in a personalized cup of potting soil and record the date in the blank. Place each cup near a window in your classroom. Have each youngster complete the activities in his plant booklet as his seed begins to grow. You can count on "plant-y" of learning from seed to plant!

Sponge Gardens

A sponge garden is just what you need to bring smiles to your students' faces! To begin, help each youngster trim a new sponge into a desired shape. (Or precut sponges prior to the lesson.) Next have each child soak his sponge with water and then wring it out. Instruct him to place his sponge on a plastic plate. Then direct the student to sprinkle mustard seeds or bean sprouts atop his moistened sponge. He places his plate in a sunny location in the classroom; then he lightly mists his sponge with a spray bottle of water several times throughout the day. (At the end of each day, cover the plates with plastic wrap; then remove the wrap the next morning.) In about two weeks, your youngsters will have a sponge garden of sprouts!

Sensational Sunflowers

Look out! These sunflowers are blooming beauties! To make a sunflower, each youngster colors the back of a six-inch paper plate brown. Next the student uses a six-inch petal template to trace nine patterns onto sheets of yellow construction paper. She then cuts out the petals and glues them to the uncolored side of her plate as shown. When the glue has dried, the youngster cuts a stem and leaves from green construction paper, then glues them to the back of her plate. To complete her sunflower, she glues sunflower seeds to the front of her flower. For added enjoyment, have youngsters munch on additional sunflower seeds as they work. Then mount the completed projects on a bulletin board titled "Sensational Sunflowers."

I planted _____ _____ .
                        kind of seed

on _____ .
      date

This is what my seed looks like:

[Draw or tape a seed here.]

Write a sentence that describes your seed.

_____

A seed has different parts. These are the parts of a seed:

Write each word on a line.

Seed Coat   Root
Food Storage

Plant Book

_____ 's

3

My seed sprouted on _____ .
                        date

Now it looks like this:

Draw a picture of your plant here.

Write two sentences that describe your plant.

_____
_____
_____

2

Seeds need _____ , _____ , and _____ to grow.

Here is a record that shows how I take care of my seed.

S	M	T	W	Th	F	S

When you plant your seed, draw 🌱 in the correct ☐ .

Each time you water your seed/plant, draw a ◌ in the correct ☐ .

When your seed sprouts, draw a 🌼 in the correct ☐ .

©1998 The Education Center, Inc. • *March Monthly Reproducibles* • Grades 2–3 • TEC945

Here are three facts I have learned about plants:

1.

2.

3.

5

My plant is growing taller and taller. It has different plant parts.

Here are the parts of a plant:

Write each word on a line.

**Flower Stem Roots
Leaf Bud**

4

Note To The Teacher: Use with "Plants, Plants, Plants!" on page 35.

Your youngsters will know how to eat right after they celebrate National Nutrition Month®. Students will dig right into this collection of activities and reproducibles.

Palatable Pyramids

Introduce your youngsters to the Food Guide Pyramid with this appetizing activity. Begin by listing each food group—*Fats, Dairy, Protein, Vegetables, Fruits,* and *Grains*—vertically on the chalkboard. Ask students to name foods that belong in each group; then list their responses beside each corresponding food group. Next provide each youngster with a copy of the Food Guide Pyramid on page 40. After reviewing each named food group, tell your students that a certain number of servings is required each day. Then have each youngster select food items from each list to illustrate on his Food Guide Pyramid. Once students have illustrated each food group, direct each youngster to write a few sentences about why it is important to eat healthful, nutritious meals every day. Encourage students to refer to their Food Guide Pyramids frequently to ensure that they are eating healthful meals.

What Did I Eat?

Once youngsters have a good understanding of the Food Guide Pyramid, have each child keep track of his daily servings with a weekly food log. To make a food log, a youngster staples five copies of the food log pattern (page 41) between a folded sheet of construction paper. Next he writes "[Child's name]'s Food Log" and draws desired decorations on the front cover; then he labels the top of each page with a different day of the week. To use his log, he records the food items he eats each day in the space provided. Then he determines the total number of servings he consumed by making a tally on the Food Guide Pyramid. At the end of the week, ask each student to evaluate what he ate daily. If desired, serve students a healthful snack, like orange wedges or apple slices, as they discuss their findings.

When I came home, there was a giant peanut-butter sandwich...

Now That's A Sandwich!

Now that youngsters have built up an appetite, have them use their imaginations in this delicious writing activity. Invite students to name their favorite kinds of sandwiches. Then ask each child to imagine what it might be like if she came home from school one day and found a giant-sized version of her favorite sandwich in the backyard. Have her write a story about her experience on a copy of the bread pattern on page 42. Provide time for each student to share her story with her classmates. Then collect the stories and bind them between two bread-shaped construction-paper covers. Add the title "Now That's A Sandwich!" to the front cover, and place the booklet in the reading center for students to enjoy again and again!

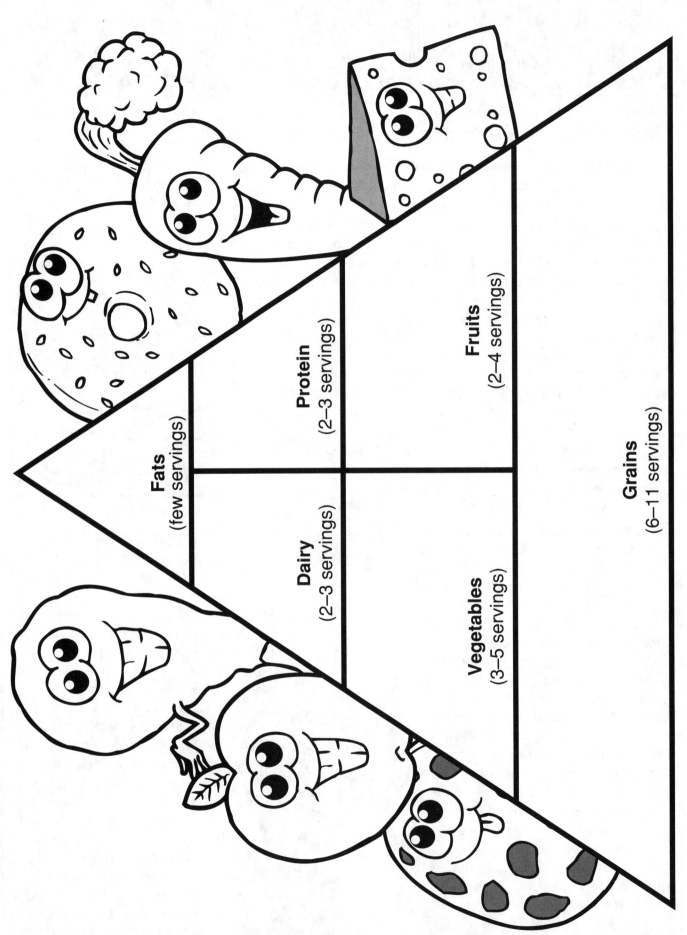

Fats
(few servings)

Protein
(2–3 servings)

Dairy
(2–3 servings)

Fruits
(2–4 servings)

Vegetables
(3–5 servings)

Grains
(6–11 servings)

Food Log Pages

Food Log For: _____
(date)

Today I ate:

_____
_____
_____
_____
_____
_____
_____
_____

I had:

(Count the total number of servings. Make a tally to show how many.)

Fats (sparingly)

Dairy (2–3 servings)

Protein (2–3 servings)

Vegetables (3–5 servings)

Fruits (2–4 servings)

Grains (6–11 servings)

I did/did not eat my daily servings.
(Circle *did* or *did not*.)

Food Log For: _____
(date)

Today I ate:

_____
_____
_____
_____
_____
_____
_____
_____

I had:

(Count the total number of servings. Make a tally to show how many.)

Fats (sparingly)

Dairy (2–3 servings)

Protein (2–3 servings)

Vegetables (3–5 servings)

Fruits (2–4 servings)

Grains (6–11 servings)

I did/did not eat my daily servings.
(Circle *did* or *did not*.)

Note To The Teacher: Use with "What Did I Eat?" on page 39.

Bread Pattern

Note To The Teacher: Use with "Now That's A Sandwich!" on page 39.

Name _____

Yum! Yum! Yum!

Add the missing punctuation mark to the end of each sentence.
Each time you add a punctuation mark, color a matching triangle.

1. Do I smell fresh strawberries

2. Boy, I love strawberry jam

3. I could eat it on toast every day

4. When will the jam be ready

5. Wow, this jam is delicious

△! △! △? △? △. △.

6. Ham and onions are yummy

7. I like to eat them on pizza

8. Boy, do I love pizza

9. Do you like pizza as much as I do

10. Gee, I hope you do

△! △! △? △? △. △.

11. Oh no, that grape fell on the floor

12. Did you pick it up

13. I like to eat grapes for breakfast

14. I mix them with peaches in a bowl

15. Do you like grapes or peaches

△! △! △? △? △. △.

Bonus Box: On the back of this sheet, write three sentences about your favorite nutritious snack. Write one statement, one question, and one exclamation; then flip your paper over and color the matching triangle.

Fantastic Fruit Bowl

Cut out the boxes at the bottom of the page.
Glue them in ABC order on the fruit bowl.

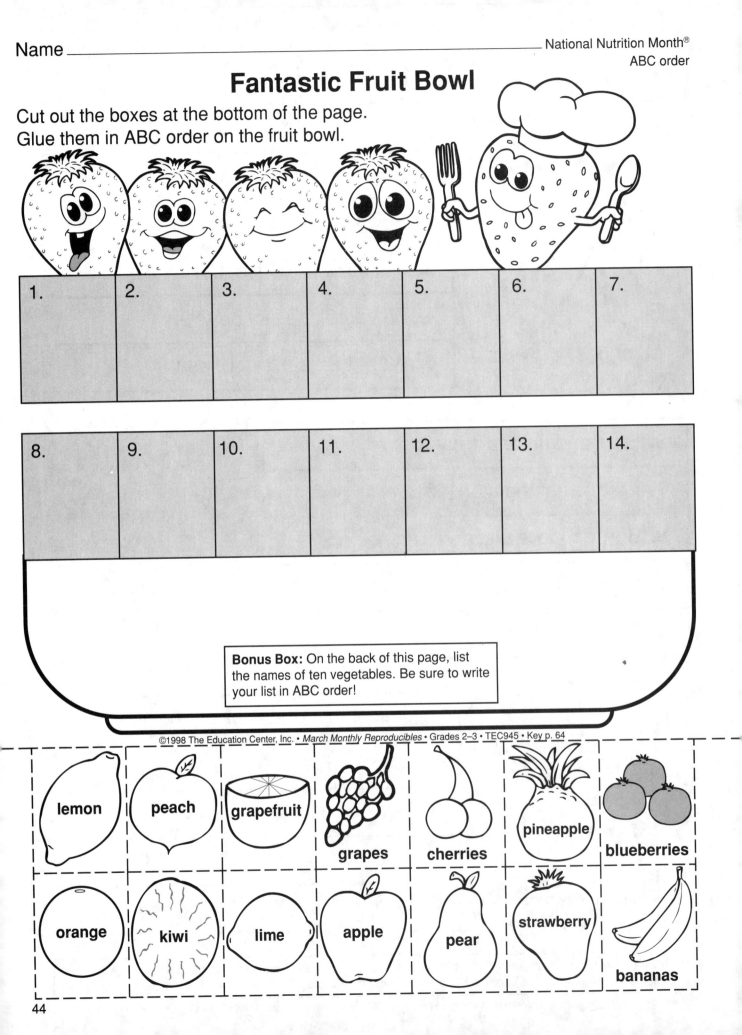

1.	2.	3.	4.	5.	6.	7.

8.	9.	10.	11.	12.	13.	14.

Bonus Box: On the back of this page, list the names of ten vegetables. Be sure to write your list in ABC order!

lemon   peach   grapefruit   grapes   cherries   pineapple   blueberries

orange   kiwi   lime   apple   pear   strawberry   bananas

National Women's History Month

Over the years, women have proven their worth in history. Introduce your youngsters to some of these strong and courageous ladies when you celebrate National Women's History Month in March.

Women Wonders

This booklet project is a great way to teach youngsters about women of wonder. Duplicate one copy of page 46 and page 47 for each student. To make her booklet, a youngster cuts apart her pages and staples them in order between a folded sheet of construction paper. Then she decorates her booklet as desired. After each student has a booklet, divide students into small groups. Have each group discuss the facts about each woman. Encourage each youngster to also name things she may have in common with one or more of the ladies in her booklet. If desired, have her write about her favorite woman on writing paper. Collect the stories and display them on a bulletin board titled "Women Wonders."

A Helping Hand

Encourage students to lend a helping hand when you introduce them to Clara Barton. To begin, tell students that Clara Barton, a former schoolteacher and Civil War nurse, was noted for her lobby to form the first American branch of the Red Cross. Clara's desire to help people was evident through her actions. Tell students that they, too, can be like Clara by helping one another every day. Have each youngster write four ways she is helpful on a copy of the cross pattern (page 48). Then have her cut out the pattern, glue it to a sheet of red construction paper, and trim the paper around the pattern to create a border. Now that's a great reminder to always help one another!

> I read books for my granny.
>
> I wash the dishes on Sunday.
>
> **I help people whenever I can.**
>
> I walk the dog every day.
>
> **Four ways I have helped people are...**
>
> I clean up my room every night.

Women Champions

Have youngsters create new cereals to honor women athletes. Divide students into pairs. Assign each pair a different woman athlete from the list shown. (More than one pair may be assigned the same woman.) Have each pair research the athlete and write a few lines about her on a sheet of writing paper. Next provide each pair with a square of 12-inch poster board. Direct each pair to draw a picture on the poster board of the athlete performing her sport and illustrate it as desired. Instruct the partners to create a new name for the cereal in honor of the athlete and write it at the top of the picture. To complete the project, have each pair attach its sentences to the bottom of the poster board. Then suspend the projects from the ceiling for all to enjoy.

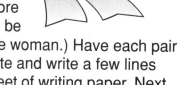

Women Athletes
Bonnie Blair
Chris Evert
Peggy Fleming
Dorothy Hamill
Jackie Joyner-Kersee
Billie Jean King
Nancy Lopez
Wilma Rudolph
Kristi Yamaguchi
Babe Didrikson Zaharias

Booklet Pages

Susan B. Anthony
1820–1906

Susan B. Anthony was one of the first ladies to fight for women's rights. She helped women get the right to vote.

1

Elizabeth Blackwell
1821–1910

Elizabeth Blackwell attended Geneva College in Geneva, New York. She became the first U.S. woman to earn a medical degree.

2

Aretha Franklin
1942–

Aretha Franklin is one of the best-selling female recording artists. She is known as the "Queen Of Soul."

3

Emily Dickinson
1830–1886

Emily Dickinson was born in Amherst, Massachusetts. She was a famous American poet.

4

Georgia O'Keeffe
1887–1986

Georgia O'Keeffe was born in Sun Prairie, Wisconsin. She studied art at many schools. She was well known for her flower paintings.

5

Jackie Joyner-Kersee
1962–

Jackie Joyner-Kersee was born in East St. Louis, Illinois. She became the first woman to win consecutive heptathlon championships.

6

Amelia Earhart
1897–1937

Amelia Earhart was an American aviator. She was the first woman to cross the Atlantic by air. She was also the first woman to receive the Distinguished Flying Cross.

7

Cynthia Rylant
1954–

Cynthia Rylant grew up in the mountains of West Virginia. She is a well-known author and illustrator of children's books.

8

Note To The Teacher: Use with "Women Wonders" on page 45.

Cross Pattern

_____
_____
_____
_____

_____   # I help people   _____
_____   # whenever I can.   _____
_____   _____
_____   # Four ways I   _____
                                   # have helped
                                   # people are...

_____
_____
_____
_____

Note To The Teacher: Use with "A Helping Hand" on page 45.

YOUTH ART MONTH

Youth Art Month falls during the month of March. Invite your youngsters to participate in these colorful activities. Before you know it, your students will have become budding young artists!

An Artist Is...

Introduce your youngsters to life as an artist. Invite a local artist to visit your classroom to speak to your youngsters about his or her career and share some works of art. Have students ask the artist prepared questions. After the visit, invite youngsters to brainstorm words that describe what an artist does. Write their responses on the chalkboard. Next have each student copy and complete the sentence "If I were an artist, I would…" on a sheet of writing paper. Direct him to incorporate some of the words from the list into his writing. Next have him illustrate a picture of himself as an artist and attach it to his story. As a finale to the activity, invite each student to don a beretlike artist's cap as he shares his story with his classmates.

If I were an artist, I would paint lots of pictures. I would wear a cap and use a palette. I would paint clouds. I would also paint different kinds of people and animals.

Breyanna

Gallery Of Art

This gallery of art is just what you need to inspire any young artist. Explain to your students that a *gallery* is a room or a building used to display art. Tell them that they will be creating works of art to display in a classroom gallery. Distribute one white construction-paper copy of the picture frame (page 50) to each student. Instruct each child to lightly pencil a picture inside her frame; then have her use crayons or colored pencils to color her picture. Next have each child decorate the border of the picture before cutting it out. Have each youngster use a black fine-tip marker to sign her work of art. Invite each student to share her masterpiece with her classmates. Collect the projects; then mount them on a rectangular bulletin board or large wall with the title "Our Gallery Of Art."

Buckets And Brushes

Create a fun learning center for students to enjoy during your celebration of Youth Art Month. Make multiple copies of the patterns on page 51. Program each bucket with a word problem; an addition or a subtraction problem; a contraction; or a word to review a particular skill, such as a synonym, an antonym, or a homophone. Then program each paintbrush with the corresponding answer. Color and cut out the pieces; then laminate them for durability. Place the pieces in a learning center. To use the center, a student selects a bucket and matches it to the correct paintbrush.

soft

hard

13 + 8

21

couldn't

could not

Picture Frame

Note To The Teacher: Use with "Gallery Of Art" on page 49.

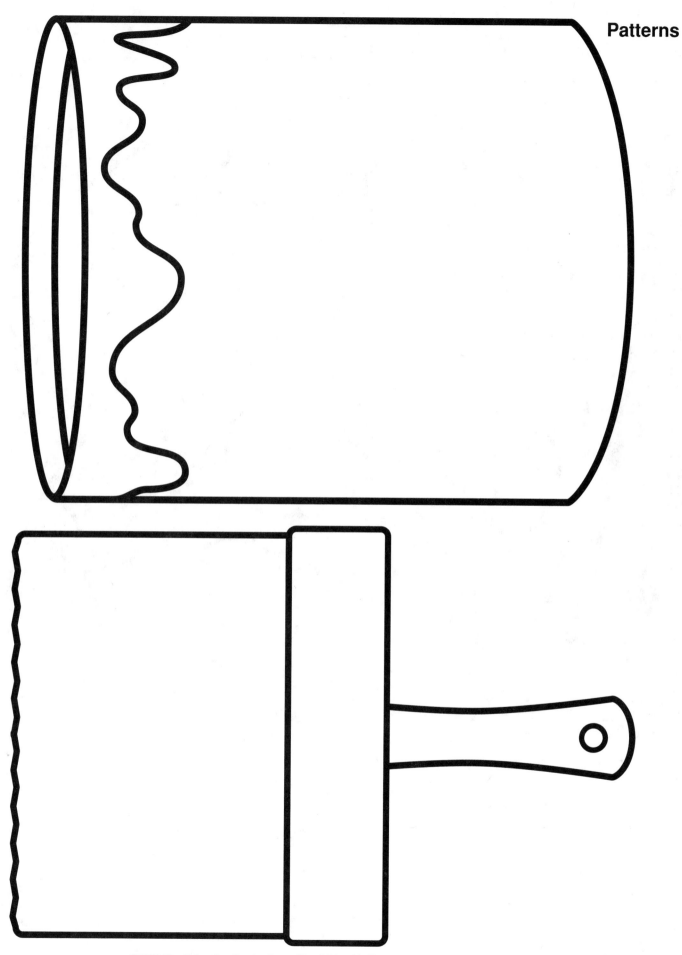

Note To The Teacher: Use with "Buckets And Brushes" on page 49.

51

Plentiful Palette

Solve the problem on each paint splotch.
Color by the code.

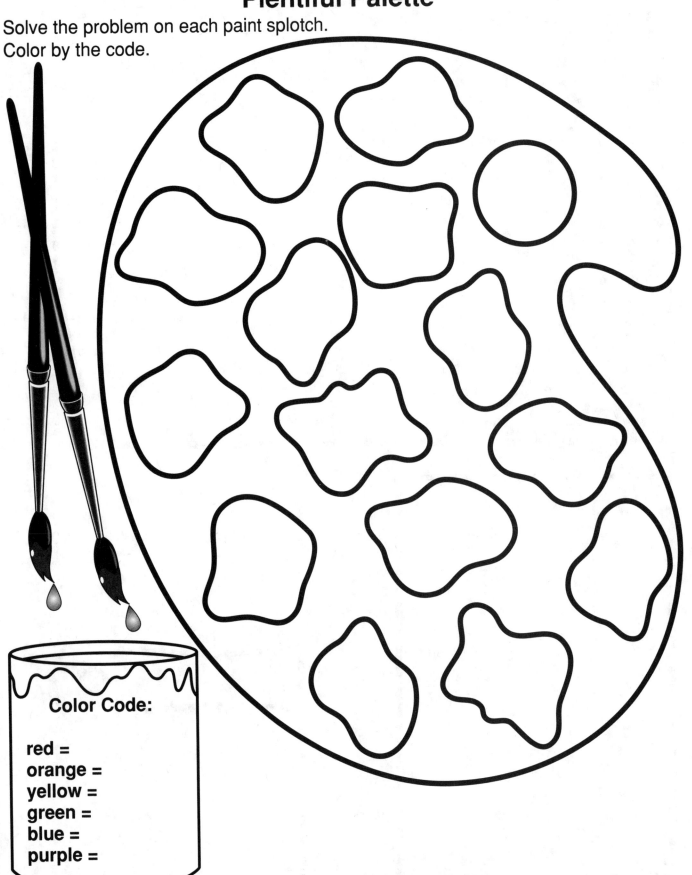

Color Code:

red =
orange =
yellow =
green =
blue =
purple =

Note To The Teacher: Program the paint splotches with addition or subtraction problems; then program the color code. Make copies of
the page for students to complete.

NATIONAL PIG DAY

Celebrate National Pig Day on March 1. Your youngsters will go hog-wild as they learn about this intelligent, useful, and domesticated animal!

Piggy Ponderings

Begin your study of pigs by sharing these "swine-tastic" facts about them!

- Pigs are intelligent animals. Among hoofed animals, pigs are one of the best problem solvers.
- *Hog* and *swine* are other names for pigs.
- A *boar* is a male pig. A *sow* is a female pig.
- Pigs in a group are called a *herd.*
- A *litter* is a name given to a group of newborn pigs.
- On warm days, pigs like to *wallow,* or roll, in mud to keep cool.
- Sows can weigh more than 450 pounds when fully grown. Boars can weigh more than *500* pounds!
- Pigs use their snouts to *root,* or dig, for vegetable roots, their favorite food.
- Pigs have 34 or 44 teeth in their mouths, depending on the species. Some of these teeth are called *tusks.* A pig uses its tusks for digging and as weapons against other animals.
- Humans eat most of the pig, and the parts that are not eaten are used to make medicines, brushes, soap, glue, and leather.

Piggy Practice

Provide piles of piggy practice for your students when you make this fun learning center! Duplicate and cut out a supply of the pig patterns on page 54. Write a money amount on the front of each pig. Use coin stamps and an ink pad to stamp the corresponding amount in coins on the back. Then laminate the pigs for durability. Place the pigs and a set of coins at a learning center. To use the center, a student selects a pig card, makes the correct amount with coins, and flips the card to check his work. Or a student may count the coins on each card, then flip the card to check his answer. Duplicate additional sets of cards and program them with addition or subtraction problems, clocks (for time practice), word problems, or contractions and the words that make up each one. For writing practice, program each pig card with a different story starter or pig-related title.

"Piggy Tales"

Share one of these delightful "pig-tales" with your students.

- *Garth Pig Steals The Show* by Mary Rayner (Dutton Children's Books, 1993)
- *Hog-Eye* by Susan Meddaugh (Houghton Mifflin Company, 1995)
- *Piggie Pie!* by Margie Palatini (Clarion Books, 1995)
- *Pigs In The Pantry* by Amy Axelrod (Simon & Schuster Books For Young Readers, 1997)
- *Pigs On A Blanket* by Amy Axelrod (Simon & Schuster Books For Young Readers, 1996)

Pig Patterns

Note To The Teacher: See "Piggy Practice" on page 53 for ideas on using these patterns.

Name _____

Pig Land

Look at the map.
Answer the questions.
Use the key to help you.

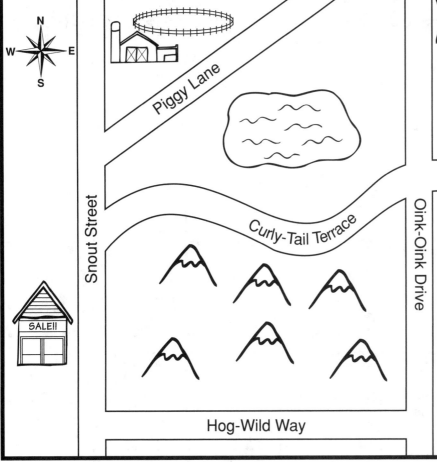

Map Key

- Petra Pig's Farm
- Swine-Mart
- Petey Pig's House
- Mud Puddle Pond
- Three Little Pigs' House
- Hoof Mountains

1. What street is Petey Pig's house on? _____

2. The Hoof Mountains are _____ of Mud Puddle Pond.
   (north, south)

3. Mud Puddle Pond is _____ of the Three Little Pigs' house.
   (east, west)

4. What roads run north and south (↕)? _____
   _____

5. What roads should Petey take to get to the Swine-Mart from his house?
   _____

6. Petey Pig's house is _____ of Petra Pig's farm.
   (east, west)

Bonus Box: Make your own map and key on the back of this paper. Write five questions for a friend to answer.

Name_____

National Pig Day
Identifying solid shapes

Swine-Mart Sort

Help Petey and Petra Pig sort their groceries by shape.
Cut out the boxes.
Glue them next to the correct grocery bags.

Cylinders				
Cubes				
Spheres				
Rectangular Prisms				

Bonus Box: Can you name any other solid shapes? Write their names on the back of this paper; then draw two pictures for each one.

©1998 The Education Center, Inc. • *March Monthly Reproducibles* • Grades 2–3 • TEC945 • Key p. 64

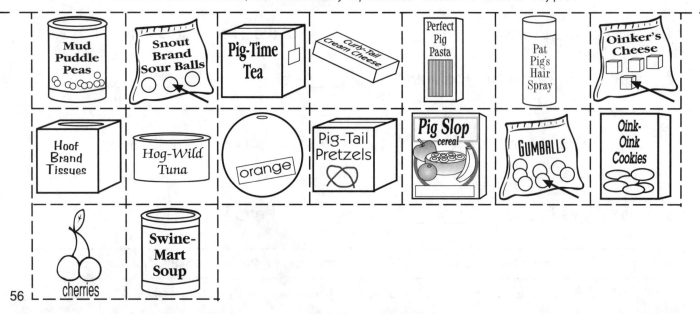

Name _____

Ready, Set...Go!

How fast can these three little piggies collect corn kernels?
Have your partner time you.
Write each time in the space.

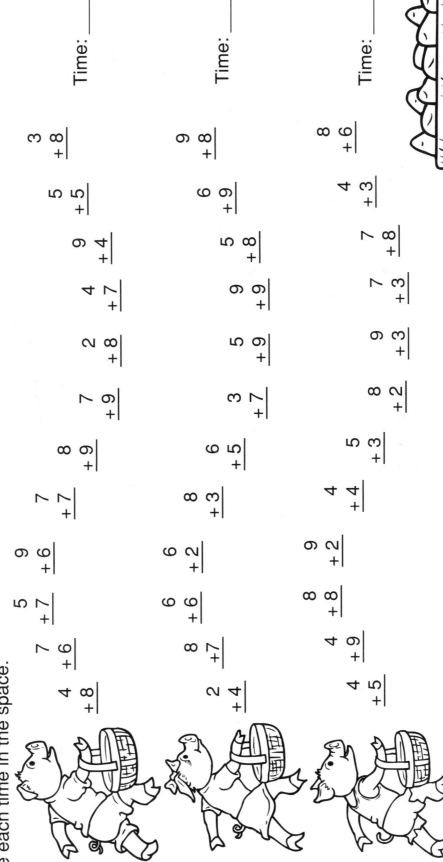

$$\begin{array}{c}4\\+8\\\hline\end{array}\quad\begin{array}{c}7\\+6\\\hline\end{array}\quad\begin{array}{c}5\\+7\\\hline\end{array}\quad\begin{array}{c}9\\\\\hline\end{array}\quad\begin{array}{c}7\\+7\\\hline\end{array}\quad\begin{array}{c}8\\+9\\\hline\end{array}\quad\begin{array}{c}7\\+9\\\hline\end{array}\quad\begin{array}{c}9\\+4\\\hline\end{array}\quad\begin{array}{c}5\\+5\\\hline\end{array}\quad\begin{array}{c}3\\+8\\\hline\end{array}$$

Time: _____

$$\begin{array}{c}2\\+4\\\hline\end{array}\quad\begin{array}{c}8\\+7\\\hline\end{array}\quad\begin{array}{c}6\\+6\\\hline\end{array}\quad\begin{array}{c}6\\+2\\\hline\end{array}\quad\begin{array}{c}8\\+3\\\hline\end{array}\quad\begin{array}{c}6\\+5\\\hline\end{array}\quad\begin{array}{c}3\\+7\\\hline\end{array}\quad\begin{array}{c}5\\+9\\\hline\end{array}\quad\begin{array}{c}9\\+9\\\hline\end{array}\quad\begin{array}{c}5\\+8\\\hline\end{array}\quad\begin{array}{c}6\\+9\\\hline\end{array}\quad\begin{array}{c}9\\+8\\\hline\end{array}$$

Time: _____

$$\begin{array}{c}4\\+5\\\hline\end{array}\quad\begin{array}{c}4\\+9\\\hline\end{array}\quad\begin{array}{c}8\\+8\\\hline\end{array}\quad\begin{array}{c}9\\+2\\\hline\end{array}\quad\begin{array}{c}4\\+4\\\hline\end{array}\quad\begin{array}{c}5\\+3\\\hline\end{array}\quad\begin{array}{c}8\\+2\\\hline\end{array}\quad\begin{array}{c}9\\+3\\\hline\end{array}\quad\begin{array}{c}7\\+3\\\hline\end{array}\quad\begin{array}{c}7\\+8\\\hline\end{array}\quad\begin{array}{c}4\\+3\\\hline\end{array}\quad\begin{array}{c}8\\+6\\\hline\end{array}$$

Time: _____

Hint:
The lowest time
is the fastest!

Use the answer key to check your answers.
For each incorrect answer, add one second to your time in that race.
If all answers are correct, subtract three seconds from your time in that race.

©1998 The Education Center, Inc. • *March Monthly Reproducibles* • Grades 2–3 • TEC945 • Key p. 64

Note To The Teacher: Duplicate one copy of the answer key on page 64 for each student.

Name _____

Mud Puddle Madness

Who will win the race?
Have your partner time you.
Write your time at the end of each race.

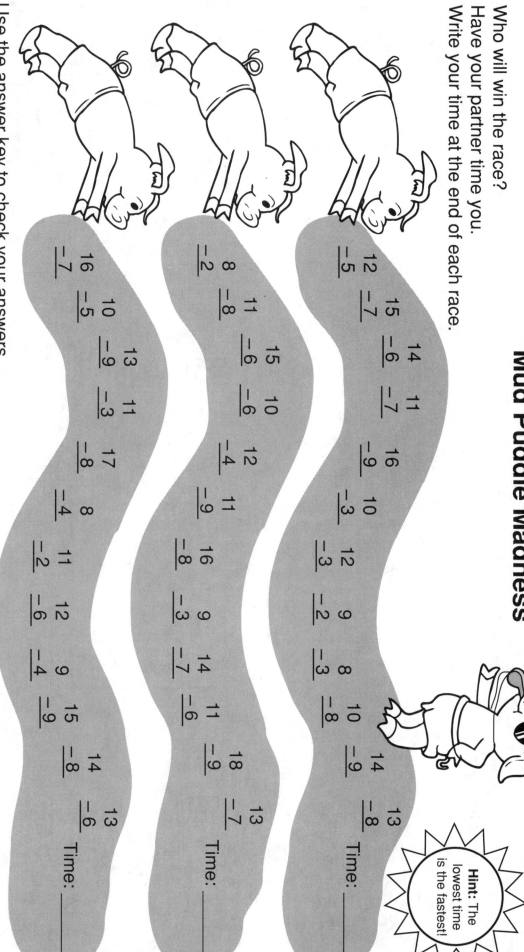

Hint: The lowest time is the fastest!

Row 1 (pig 1):
12 −5   14 −6   11 −7   16 −9   10 −3   12 −3   9 −2   8 −3   10 −8   14 −9   13 −8   Time: _____

Row 2 (pig 2):
8 −2   11 −6   15 −6   10 −6   12 −4   11 −9   16 −8   9 −3   14 −7   11 −6   18 −9   13 −7   Time: _____

Row 3 (pig 3):
16 −7   10 −5   13 −9   11 −3   17 −8   8 −4   11 −2   12 −6   9 −4   15 −9   14 −8   13 −6   Time: _____

Use the answer key to check your answers.
For each incorrect answer, add one second to that time.
If all answers are correct, subtract three seconds from that time.

©1998 The Education Center, Inc. • *March Monthly Reproducibles* • Grades 2–3 • TEC945 • Key p. 64

Note To The Teacher: Duplicate one copy of the answer key on page 64 for each student.

NEWSPAPER IN EDUCATION WEEK

Celebrate Newspaper In Education Week, annually the first full week in March. It won't be long before your newshounds will be sniffing out their next scoop!

Newspaper Scavenger Hunt

Review basic skills by having students hunt through a newspaper. In advance, write a list of scavenger-hunt items on sheets of paper. (Vary the items on each list to provide students with even more practice.) Each list can include specific newspaper-related items, like a headline, a particular comic, or an editorial. Or you may choose to have students hunt for words that review a learned skill, such as words that contain the *st* blend.

To begin the hunt, divide students into small groups. Provide each group with a copy of a newspaper and a scavenger-hunt list. Set a time limit and let the fun begin! Challenge each group to hunt for its list of specific items in the newspaper and check them off as they are found. When time has expired, reward the group that found the most items with a sticker or another small treat. For even more fun, have groups swap lists and hunt for items again!

Hot Off The Press!

This one-of-a-kind newsletter will have your students in-the-know with newspapers. To begin, share several newspapers with your students. Help youngsters understand that it takes many different jobs to get a newspaper published. Tell students that one such job is that of *reporter.* Explain that the reporter is the one who gathers the information needed to write a story. He tells *who, what, where, when,* and *why.* The *editor* then checks the story before it appears in the newspaper. Next tell your students that they will be working together as reporters to help create a classroom newspaper.

First pair students; then distribute one copy of the "Newshound Notes" (page 60) to each pair. Assign each pair a topic, such as Classroom Highlights, Reminders For Parents, Special Thanks, Help Wanted, or Hats Off To A Special Student(s). (The same topic may be assigned to more than one pair.) Each pair gathers information about its topic, then records the information on its Newshound Notes. Next the pair uses the information to write a story. Collect the stories and use the information to program a copy of the classroom newsletter on page 61. Send home copies of the newsletter for your newshounds to share with their families.

#1 Newshounds!

Conclude your celebration of Newspaper In Education Week by rewarding your newshounds with a special award. Duplicate one copy of the certificate pattern (page 62) onto colorful paper for each student. Program each certificate with a child's name, your signature, and the date; then present one to each child in your class. Now that's a special delivery each child is sure to remember.

Newshound Notes
Reported by

_____

Who? _____
_____

What? _____
_____

Where? _____
_____

When? _____
_____

Why? _____
_____

Other notes: _____
_____
_____

Newshound Notes
Reported by

_____

Who? _____
_____

What? _____
_____

Where? _____
_____

When? _____
_____

Why? _____
_____

Other notes: _____
_____
_____

©1998 The Education Center, Inc. • _March Monthly Reproducibles_ • Grades 2–3 • TEC945

60   **Note To The Teacher:** Use with "Hot Off The Press!" on page 59.

HOT OFF THE PRESS

Teacher: _____   Date: _____

Highlights

Hats Off To...

Reminders

Special Thanks

Help Wanted

Note To The Teacher: Use with "Hot Off The Press!" on page 59.

Certificates

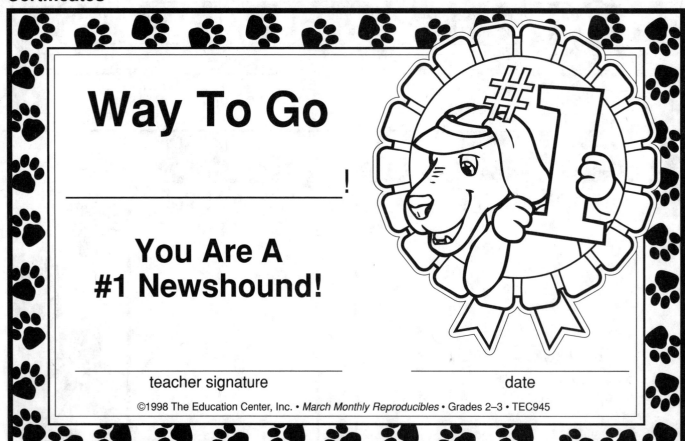

Way To Go

_____ !

You Are A #1 Newshound!

_____   _____
teacher signature   date

©1998 The Education Center, Inc. • *March Monthly Reproducibles* • Grades 2–3 • TEC945

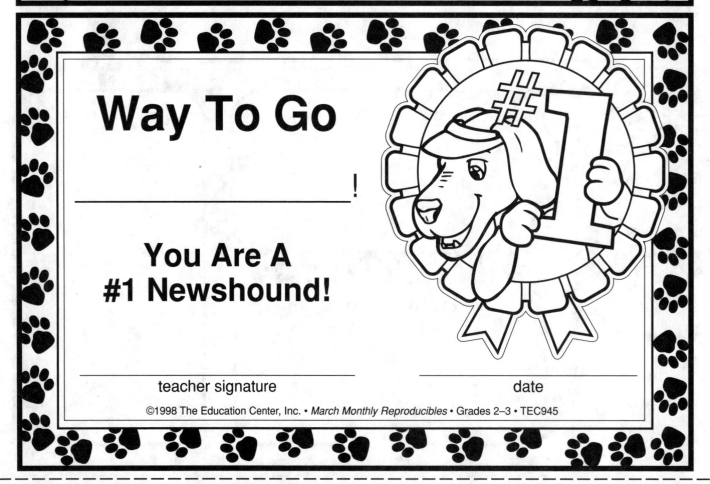

Way To Go

_____ !

You Are A #1 Newshound!

_____   _____
teacher signature   date

©1998 The Education Center, Inc. • *March Monthly Reproducibles* • Grades 2–3 • TEC945

Note To The Teacher: Use with "#1 Newshounds!" on page 59.

Answer Keys

Page 9
Answers on tree will be crossed out.

433 + 466 899	157 + 725 882	423 + 328 751	832 + 158 990	
126 + 835 961	575 + 127 702	264 + 508 772	415 + 555 970	
555 + 156 711	438 + 529 967	637 + 236 873	264 + 196 460	362 + 549 911
172 + 598 770	416 + 217 633	578 + 239 817	319 + 345 664	376 + 454 830
688 + 155 843	493 + 199 692	827 + 147 974	385 + 195 580	267 + 276 543
	459 + 462 921	348 + 638 986	495 + 235 730	

Page 10
Answers on bushes will be crossed out.

405 − 217 188	702 − 335 367	602 − 327 275		
303 − 144 159	307 − 198 109	402 − 387 15		
101 − 75 26	507 − 138 369	104 − 47 57	906 − 88 818	604 − 165 439
705 − 499 206	806 − 568 238	605 − 218 387	905 − 36 869	406 − 329 77
204 − 126 78	707 − 358 349	802 − 496 306	203 − 58 145	901 − 454 447
		503 − 276 227	808 − 319 489	502 − 244 258

Page 12
1. polite   lost   hard
2. float   down   tiny
3. thin   out   sour
4. bad   walk   cold
5. poor   stop   quiet

Page 13

Page 14
1. 85¢	2. 50¢	3. 45¢	4. 92¢
5. 89¢	6. 95¢	7. 90¢	8. 79¢
9. 73¢	10. 63¢	11. 72¢	12. 93¢

Page 15
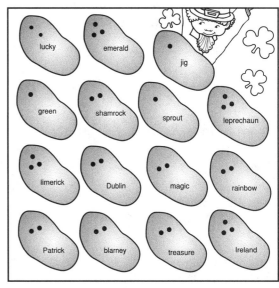

Page 23
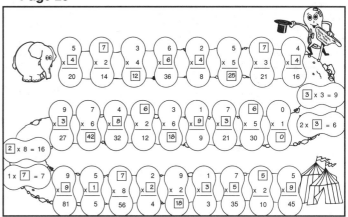

Page 24
1. coin
2. knight
3. peep
4. taught
5. gleam
6. find
7. spring
8. main
9. tickle
10. brown
11. groom
12. stair
13. power
14. spread
15. float
16. cable

Page 26
Order of kite tails may vary.

12	**15**	**14**
6 + 6	8 + 7	6 + 8
8 + 4	6 + 9	9 + 5
9 + 3	10 + 5	10 + 4
7 + 5	11 + 4	7 + 7

Answer Keys

Page 28
1. It was a sunny and windy day.
2. Meg and Tim asked their mom if they could fly a kite outside.
3. Meg and Tim got the kite out of the garage.
4. They took the kite to the park.
5. Meg held the kite, while Tim let out the string.
6. Meg let go of the kite as Tim started to run.
7. The wind caught the kite.
8. The kite flew high in the air.

Page 29
1. 1:30 2. 4:00 3. 7:30 4. 12:00
5. 6:30 6. 9:00 7. 11:30 8. 2:00
9. 3:30 10. 5:00

Page 33
1. 39   2. 75¢   3. 31
4. 28   5. 27   6. 8
7. 52   8. 50¢   9. 24
10. 46¢

Page 34
blow	bubble	gumball	sticky
chewy	pink	pop	soft
brand	candy	cinnamon	wrapper
messy	minty	super	tasty

Page 43
1. ?   9. ?
2. !   10. !
3. .   11. !
4. ?   12. ?
5. !   13. .
6. .   14. .
7. .   15. ?
8. !

Page 44

Page 55
1. Oink-Oink Drive
2. south
3. west
4. Snout Street and Oink-Oink Drive
5. Oink-Oink Drive to Curly-Tail Terrace to Snout Street or Oink-Oink Drive to Hog-Wild Way to Snout Street
6. east

Page 56
Order will vary.

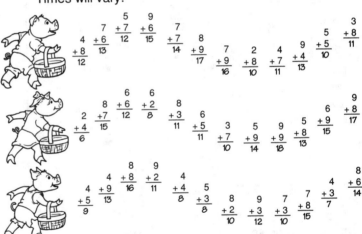

Page 57
Times will vary.

Page 58
Times will vary.

64